Zig Misiak: Author
Jennifer Bettio: Illustrator
Raymond R. Skye, Tuscarora/Seneca, Grand River Six Nations Territory:
Contributor of Six Nations art and stories.

Revised Edition, 2021, ISBN 978-0-9950128-1-3

All Publications by Zig Misiak

FIRST NATIONS RESOURCE COLLECTION, ISBN 978-0-9811880-2-7
WAMPUM: The Story of Shaylyn the Clam, ISBN-978-0-9811880-8-9
WAR of 1812: Highlighting Native Nations, ISBN 978-0-9811880-5-8
WAR of 1812: Western Hooves of Thunder, ISBN 978-0-9811880-3-4
TONTO: The Man in Front of the Mask, ISBN 978-0-9811880-6-5
4 in 1 LEARNING: French & English, ISBN 978-0-9950128-0-6
ABC's Colouring Book, ISBN 978-0-9950128-9-9
1-2-3's, Shapes & Colours Colouring Book, ISBN 978-1-7771417-0-7
ASHER: of the Heron Clan, ISBN 978-0-9950128-3-7
COLTON: of the Bear Clan, ISBN 978-8-9950128-2-0
CRISTINE: of the Snipe Clan, ISBN 978-0-9950128-7-5
DARYL: of the Deer Clan, ISBN 978-0-9950128-6-8
LUKE: of the Eel Clan, ISBN 978-1-7771417-7-6
MEAGHAN: of the Hawk Clan, ISBN 978-0-9950128-8-2
RYAN: of the Wolf Clan, ISBN 978-0-9950128-5-1
STANLEY: of the Beaver Clan, ISBN 978-1-7771417-8-3
TYLER: of the Turtle Clan, ISBN 978-0-9950128-1-3
POLISH Heritage Guide, ISBN 978-1-7771417-5-2

www.canadianauthoreducation.com

About Clans

All **First Nations, Métis and Inuit People**, similar to other nations around the world, have a family system. The First Nations Métis, and Inuit people are interwoven with nature like interdependent fibres in the colourful and mysterious tapestry of life.

Clans existed well before Europeans came to **Turtle Island**, known to many as North America. In the world of the **Haudenosaunee**, also known as the Six Nations or Iroquois, they even existed before the coming of the **Peacemaker**.

The TURTLE, the main story in this book, is one of the nine (9) Clan animals of the Six Nations. These two introductory pages, plus the supplemental pages at the end of the story, will be informative.

Relax and get ready to enjoy the turtle's adventures around a creek as well as becoming enlightened about First Nations Clans.

9 Clans of the Haudenosaunee

Of the land	Bear	Wolf	Deer
Of the water	Eel	Beaver	Turtle
Of the air	Heron	Snipe	Hawk

Other examples of First Nations animals and relations.

West Coast Haida
They belong to one of two groups of Clans, the Eagle or the Raven.

Anishinaabe Clans
Bear, Otter, Fish, Eagle, Loon, Crane, Deer.

Mikmaq Spirit Animals
Bear, Lynx, Beaver, Crow, Eagle, Fox, Moose, Wolf.

The Young Man and the Clans

The **Young Man** noticed that there was a lack of support between people, especially when they were grieving. He spoke to the elders saying that all of nature worked in harmony and that humans needed to get back into that harmonious natural rhythm.

He was permitted to unfold his plan. First he had all the elder women of each family find and observe an animal they were drawn too. Over some time the women came back to him with their choices. He assigned those particular animals to each unit giving them that animals name.

He then had all the people gather at the river. There he divided them into two predetermined groups having one half cross to the other side.

Once everyone was settled in, the Young Man explained that the river was like the fire in their lodges that divided the mothers and father sides of the family.

He said, "Let the fire symbolize the division the river created. Let the Clans support and address each other across the fire in the longhouses. During times of loss the related Clans on the opposite side will console and lend assistance to those in grief."

The **Matriarchal** Clan system was born and created a strong bond amongst the Original Ones, the **Onkwehon:we**, becoming an important part of their lives, then and now.

The Young Man's concept of bringing the people together, as extended families, served them well. They worked together and continued to learn from nature, caring for it as the **Creator** had intended.

The Peacemaker

Sadly, when the Peacemaker arrived, many years later, the Clan system was dysfunctional due to the fragmentation of the Clans and constant warfare between the nations. The Peacemaker, a woman named **Jikonsaseh** and **Hayenwah:tha**, re-established the Clans creating a strong foundation for their newly organized **Confederacy** based on the **Great Law of Peace**. He told the Onkwehon:we that from now on they would also be known as the Haudenosaunee, the People Building a Longhouse.

The Stories of Creation, formation of the Clans, the coming of the Peacemaker leading to the existence of the Confederacy are all available in detail in the Six Nations Iroquois Program Teachers Resource Guide . Written by Raymond R. Skye, Tuscarora/Seneca, and collaborators, from the Grand River Six Nations Territory and related Six Nations communities.

Tyler Stanley Misiak

Our Son

Where there is water there you will find life. Oceans, lakes, rivers, creeks and ponds are all vessels containing living things. Yes, even some puddles.

Our story takes place in and around a **creek**. This creek could be any one of thousands of creeks located in the Great Lakes region.

Our narrow creek gently meanders through a forest, over rocks, cutting its way into the soft surface of rolling fields, and then melts into the wider waters of a fast flowing river.

Plants, insects and animals of every shape, size and colour co-exist here in great numbers. The air is clean, the gurgling water is fresh and crystal clear. Everything is in harmony.

It was June. Mother turtle crawled up a tiny hill, near the creek, and there she dug a shallow hole. She laid her eggs in the hole and then filled it in to keep the tiny eggs warm and safe.

In late September, all of the soft-shelled eggs began to move. They cracked open and one by one little heads popped out allowing the hatchlings to wiggle themselves into the world. At birth, turtles immediately learn how to survive on their own. Their mother provides nothing for them after they are born.

Instinctively they knew where to go. They made their way down the little hill to the gently flowing creek where they began to drink the cool water and munch on tender green plants.

Once they were full the tiny **bale** of **painted turtles** swam to a partially submerged log. Using their sharp baby claws they began to awkwardly climb up the sides of the log.

Some made it on top quite easily while others slid back into the water having to start climbing all over again. This log was a perfectly safe resting place for them as they got used to their new surroundings. Each one of them would independently decide what to do next.

Only one little turtle did not make it onto the log but stayed floating in the water alone. His name was Tyler. Tyler made his choice early and swam away from his bale.

Tyler took a deep breath and let himself sink under the water to see what was there. He came to rest on a small rock just as a tiny school of fish swam past him very quickly.

A baby **snapping turtle** was chasing them. Snapping turtles are very strong and good hunters. Normally they hide and let their prey come to them. When their prey is close enough the snapping turtles head lunges forward very quickly to catch it.

Tyler enjoyed watching the snapping turtle try, unsuccessfully, to catch the faster moving fish. The little fish, followed by the determined snapping turtle, faded into the distance.

Tyler looked up toward the surface and noticed a log floating in the **cove**. When he got to it he made his way to the top. From there he saw a beautiful carpet of green lily pads, dotted with purple flowers, growing in large patches between the log and the shore.

Birds and insects of all sizes and colours were visible everywhere. Some of them rested on plants while others playfully zigzagged in the air. Tyler was just watching and learning.

Suddenly, amid the carpet of lilies, there was a big splash of water that made Tyler's eyes open very wide. Adventurous and necessarily curios, Tyler poked his head under the water.

There he saw a young **largemouth bass.** It was swimming and dodging the water lilies long stems that grew out of the bottom of the cove. This mother bass was swimming very close to five smaller fish. They were her newborn babies. She was protecting them.

The family of bass swam away moving deeper into the forest of lily pad roots and disappeared. Tyler, not seeing anything else of interest under the water, started to swim toward the shore.

Slowly, as turtles do, Tyler began to climb up the slope of a tiny island. His body had to push aside the tall green **cattails** to get to the top. There he popped his nose and head between them to see what was on the other side.

Not only did Tyler see five other turtles, painted turtles, resting on a large pile of logs but he also saw other creatures that were quite big, round, and very furry.

The stream that Tyler was born near was wider than normal because natures architects, the **beaver**, built a dam across it. They had been hard at work for months. Inside, part of the dam was formed to be partially hollow with an underwater entrance. That is where they lived.

The beaver dam held back most of the water that would have normally flowed down stream out to the river. The damming of the water created quite a large pond for all to enjoy.

Beavers gnawed bushes and trees with their long sharp teeth then dragged the cut branches to the dam and placed them where needed. Instinctively, beavers know exactly what to do and how to do it. How do you think they know how to build so well?

Beavers have webbed feet and strong flat tails making them great swimmers. They also use their tails to make a noise, by hitting the water very hard, warning of danger approaching.

Anxious to explore more places, Tyler swam to the edge of the pond, and there dove under water to the other side of the dam. He dogged the long stems of the lily pads only to bump into a pair of long yellow legs. Looking upwards he saw a very tall and fluffy white bird.

He was between the legs of a rare white **heron**. It was standing quite still gazing into the water. Without warning, the herons long beak cut through the water barely missing Tyler.

The heron caught a fish and as quickly as its head and beak penetrated the water it pulled its head and beak back out with its prize. Tyler dove under a nearby lily pad and swam safely away from the heron finding himself in the middle of a school of **pollywogs.**

There were hundreds of them. Many still had tails and some had tiny feet. Not all the pollywogs looked the same because they were frogs in different stages of growth.

Passing through the cloud of pollywogs Tyler slowly swam toward the surface of the water and crawled on to another log.

Tyler turned his head around to see where he had come from. When he turned his head back to the front he saw a **snail** crawling ever so slowly across the pedal of a red flower.

Tyler stretched his head and neck out toward the snail. The snail pulled its head and body into its shell completely disappearing. Tyler reacted automatically and did the same thing. Now they were both hiding inside their shells.

Not many other animals or insects have shells, homes on their backs, to hide in.

The snail stayed inside its shell. Tyler had already come out of his and was moving along the log toward the shore. He climbed between the plants to the top of another mound.

Tyler stopped and glanced back to look at the snail. By now it too had come out of its shell and was drinking from a water droplet that lay on the surface of the flowers pedal.

Tyler started to walk down the small slope. It was wet and slippery. He pulled his four legs inside his shell and like a toboggan he slid gently into the pond. That must have been fun.

Tyler let himself sink underwater and began to swim looking to explore some more.

Soon, Tyler had to surface to get some more fresh air. As he moved closer to the shore he came up alongside a grey rock and there he heard a croaking sound.

The croaking was coming from a small **leopard frog**. It stopped croaking for just a second, when it spotted Tyler, but then started croaking again.

It was as if this frog had signaled all the other frogs to start croaking. Tyler heard many more frogs croaking hidden among the lily pads and on shore between the tall cattails.

They sounded like a badly tuned orchestra. Too many croaks coming from so many places.

These leopard frogs were likely some of the frogs that laid the thousands of eggs that had turned into the squiggly pollywogs that Tyler swam through earlier.

Tyler turned away from the frog near him and continued to explore. Tyler swam dowstream hugging the shore. His head stayed above the water most of the time.

Once in a while he would poke his head underwater to see what he was swimming over. He was still trying to find a place that he could call home.

Tyler was moving further away from the pond that was created by the beaver dam. He was getting closer to where his small creek flowed into the faster moving and larger river. What would he find there?

Tyler crawled on top of another small log. To his right, walking past him, were two young Native people, one boy and one girl. The girl was carrying a **fishing spear** and three fish strung on a rope. The boy was behind her and he was also carrying two freshly caught fish.

They were walking near the shore, a shallow part of the river, toward their camp. The camp was a hunting camp and a home for the hunters when they were away from their village.

The fish were cleaned, rubbed with salt, and hung to dry on a rack in the sun. Later they were taken into the **smokehouse** to dry even more. These smoked fish were then taken back to the village for the others to eat right away or store to enjoy over the winter months.

There were two **wikiups** in this hunting camp. One wikiup was used as their shelter and the other was a smokehouse used to smoke and preserve the fish.

Tyler relaxed on his log for quite some time watching the two young Natives fish and prepare their catch. When they disappeared into their wikiup to rest, Tyler slipped off the log and swam underwater toward the opposite side of the river.

Swimming past a mallard duck Tyler peered through some bulrushes and there, in front of him, he saw three **black bears.** He noticed that the Natives on the other side of the river were not bothered by the bears and the bears did not seem to be bothered by them. They were all minding their own business and just fishing and going about their lives.

There were two bear cubs and one mother bear. She had caught a fish and was bringing it to the cubs to eat. One of the cubs was interested in the fish but the other was busy watching and playing with a **crayfish.** The crayfish, Tyler thought, did not seem to be enjoying itself.

Near the bears, hanging from a tree branch, was a beehive. The bees were collecting pollen and nectar from the nearby flowers. The nectar was brought back to the hive for food and for making honey.

Bears like honey very much but today, except for one cub, they were interested in the fish.

Tyler slid under the water and started to swim back toward the area of the beaver dam and the pond. It was a long journey but he was in no hurry. He was having a great time.

When Tyler arrived at the beaver dam he dove under water coming up on the other side. He moved toward the shore among the lily pads where he saw two large **Canada geese.** The geese, without any further interest, glanced at him then turned away.

Winter was approaching and the geese were flying south. They had come from as far north as the Arctic where they nested and hatched their chicks. Millions of geese were traveling thousands of miles south to the United States and northern Mexico.

This small flock of twenty three geese arrived at the pond in a **V-formation**. Stopping here to rest and eat, some of them landed on the shore and others landed smoothly on top of the water. Others, landing awkwardly, made loud complaining honking noises.

There were so many activities for Tyler to watch. A few of the geese were dunking their heads underwater catching tiny minnows while others were eating fresh plants. Some geese just waddling around doing nothing but honk.

Suddenly the honking stopped. Then they all started to honk together. This was a signal for them to leave. They flapped their large wings and slowly rose into the air. As they flew higher they began forming a big circle. When they were all up they moved closer together.

Tyler watched as they finally gathered in their pre-arranged traveling V-formation. The stronger ones were always up front. They were on their way south again.

Tyler's little nose stuck out of the water. A purple **dragonfly** thought it to be a good place to land and rest. Tyler, being very still, just stared at it with his eyes crossed holding his breath.

Dragonflies have two sets of wings that give them great mobility. They can hover, move in circles and bolt side to side quickly. They are one of the fastest insects that live around water. In a flash the dragonfly zipped off and disappeared among the bulrushes.

Winter was coming soon. Tyler had to **hibernate.** Turtles store food and can absorb all the oxygen they need through their bodies to survive until spring. Tyler found a suitable spot, among the plants, where he could soon burrow and snuggle in for the winter.

The bottom of the pond got cold but did not reach freezing temperatures that could hurt Tyler. In the spring Tyler would awake, surface, and certainly look for more adventures.

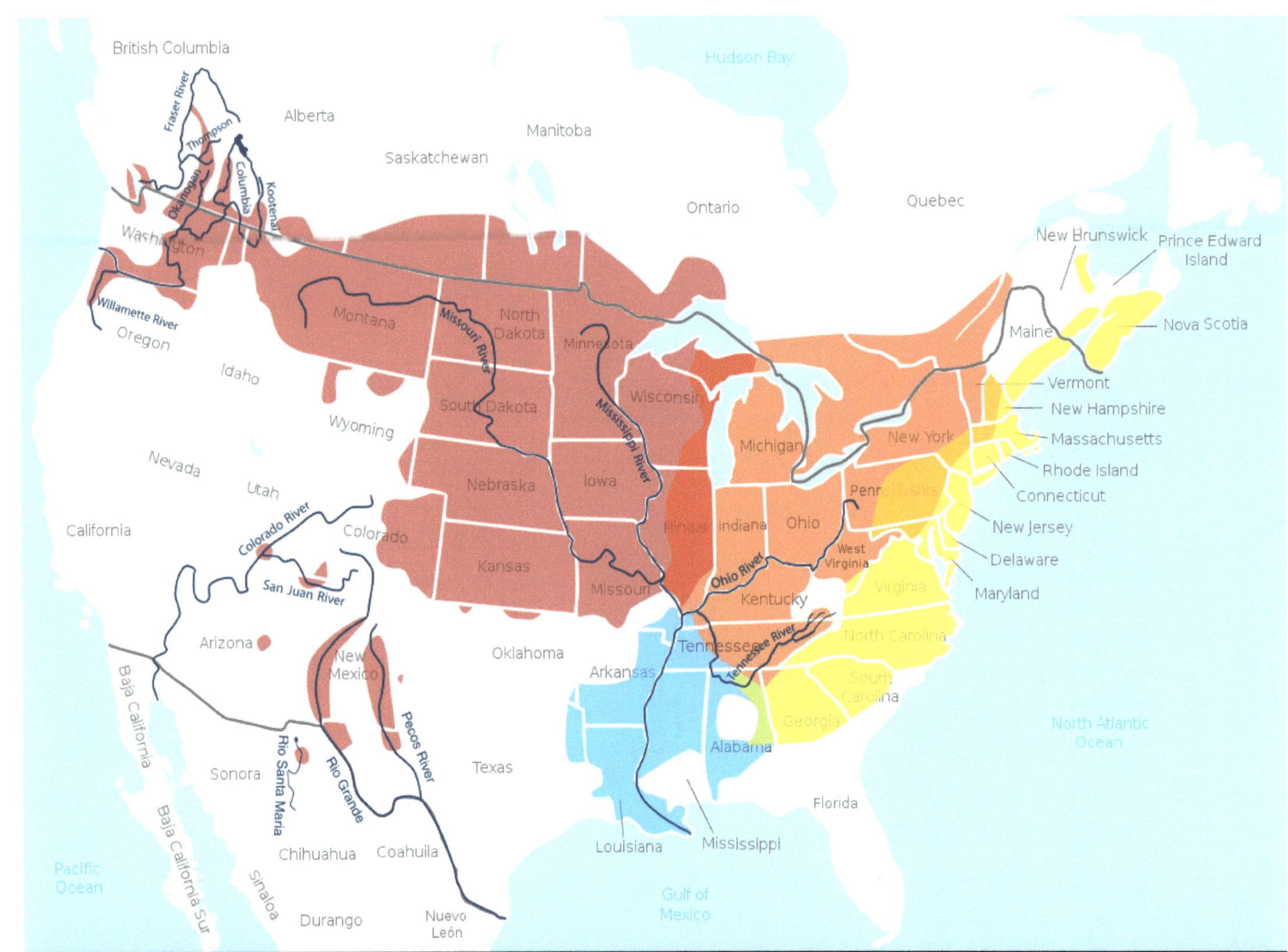

Range of Painted Turtles in North America

Yellow; Eastern **Orange**; Midland **Blue**; Southern **Red**; Western

Key Vocabulary

Bale: A group of turtles is called a bale, turn, dole, or nest.

Beaver: They are the second largest rodent in the world. They are semi-nocturnal and eat leaves, roots and bark.

Black bear: They are the smallest of the bears in North America. They can run up to 40 km/hr.

Heron: Live in colonies called rookeries. Heron fossils date back 1.8 million years. Normally blueish white, rare just white.

Canada goose: The female is called a goose, the male is called a gander and the young are called goslings.

Cattails: Are tall perennial spiky looking plants also called a bulrushes. They grow in marshy areas.

Clans: First Nations Clans are people related by a blood-line through the women. In the Haudenosaunee culture an individual would have their own personal name, belonging to the Wolf Clan of the Mohawk Nation.

Confederacy: The union of the original Five Nations under the Great Law of Peace as composed and implemented by the Peacemaker, Hayenwah:tha and Jikonsaseh. It re-established the Clan system and the Nations councils.

Crayfish: They look like tiny lobster. Fresh water crustaceans are part of the same family as lobster, shrimp and crabs.

Creator: As it is with many other nations around the world there is a Creator of all things. All First Nations, Inuit and Métis have a Creator in their stories related to the 'Beginning Times'.

Creek: Flowing water starts as a brook then flows into a stream then into a creek that drains into a river.

Dragonfly: One dragonfly can eat several hundred mosquitos a day. Take care of them.

Fishing spear: This was a traditional way of fishing using a long stick with a sharp bone pointed tip.

First Nations, Métis and Inuit People: First Nations are the 'Original People' from this part of the world. The Métis are people of mixed blood, First Nations and Euro-American. Inuit, living in northern Canada, parts of Greenland and Alaska, are not First Nations but are also 'Original People'. Indigenous, Aboriginal and Native are all words that are used interchangeably. The word 'Indian', still used in the U.S.A., is more acceptable in Canada when used in a historic context.

Great Law of Peace: It is an actual living and breathing oral, then later written, document outlining the guidelines where reason, moderation and careful discussion were informed and influenced by past events, the current situation, and the possible impact on seven generations into the future. (www.canadianauthoreducation.com)

Haudenosaunee: In the Onondaga language this means the People of the Longhouse or the Longhouse Builders. The original Five Nations Confederacy consisted of the Mohawk, Seneca, Onondaga, Oneida and Cayuga People.

Key Vocabulary

Hayenwah:tha: He was born Onondaga. He suffered greatly before coming into contact with the Peacemaker. He was crucial in assisting the Peacemaker with spreading the peace among the nations and establishing the 'Great Law of Peace'.

Hibernate: Turtles take a winter season snooze just like bears, squirrels, rodents and even rattle-snakes.

Jikonsaseh: The Peacemaker converted her from evil and she then became one of his biggest supporters spreading the 'Good Word'. She is sometimes referred to as the original Clan Mother.

Large mouth bass: Female can lay between 10,000 to 35,000 eggs per nesting.

Leopard frog: Greenish brown in colour with brown spots. A group of frogs is called an army.

Matriarchal: A system based on female lineage wherein women had great influence, control and leadership in all aspects of a particular society.

Onkwehon:we: In the Mohawk language this is translated as the 'Original People' or the 'First Ones'. Inuit also refer to themselves in this way.

Painted turtles: It is the most widespread turtle in North America. They can live up to 40 years. Turtles have existed for about 220 million years. There are 356 species of turtles world-wide.

Polliwog or tadpole: Depends on the frog/toad they come from they fully develop between 1 to 8 months.

Shadow: It is a dark shape that is formed when an object blocks a source of light. Shadows can be made during sunny days or by the use of artificial lighting. A shadow would appear on the opposite side of the object.

Smokehouse: A structure in which a fire, creating as much smoke as possible, was built to smoke and cure fish or meat.

Snail: Like an oyster and clam snails have a protective shell into which they can pull their bodies.

Snapping turtle: They can weigh anywhere from 9 to 36 lbs (4 to 6 kg), about the weight of a 3 year old child.

Turtle Island: In the Haudenosaunee creation story, a woman, Sky Woman, fell from the sky landing on a sea turtle. Over a long period of time many other land masses were formed on earth. North America is a part of Turtle Island.

V-formation: A style of flying. The first goose cuts the air and this helps the others behind fly easier.

Wikiup: Also called a wigwam they are small usually rounded structures made of bark, branches and brush.

Young Man: Inspired by the Creator, this man presented a plan to his people from which the Clan system was born.

Turtle Clan

A no:wara Ota:ra
Pronounced: A-no-wah-rah Odah-rah

Respectful, spiritual connection to the land, methodical, adaptable, peaceful

Turtle Clan people are ardent caretakers of the land, or Mother Earth as they call it. They are very compassionate, and have a deep spiritual connection to the Earth which is considered their strongest quality. Always patient and methodical, Turtle Clan members like to plan well ahead to ensure a clear, safe path. This kind of organization they trust will give them the skills and confidence they need for their journeys in life.

The Turtle Clan has always been fascinated by the turtle's endurance and longevity. They consider it a docile creature, yet admire its tenacity and courage as a strong survivor. Turtle Clan people, like the turtle, are also strong survivors who attribute their strength to faith and perseverance. They firmly believe the turtle possesses great wisdom because of its ancient origin.

This is expressed in the belief that land was created on the back of a turtle as told in the story of creation. It is why they regard the earth as their mother, for she provides life to all of creation. The Turtle Clan represents all that is sacred to Mother Earth.

Words by: Awedodyoh, Raymond R. Skye
Tuscarora * Seneca
Grand River Six Nations Territory
www.canadianauthoreducation.com

Questions & Answers

1. **What was the main purpose of the Clan?**

To create family units that would help one another through daily living but mainly for consoling during times of grief.

2. **Who played a key part in developing the Clans and how?**

The Young Man presented the idea first to the elders then he was allowed to speak to the people.

3. **How did the Clan animals help the people develop character?**

They were examples of co-operation and coexistence with nature.

4. **Who were the key players in the Clan structure and what roles did they play?**

The women, caretakers of life, watched and selected the animals they related to.

5. **How would Clan members take care of one another?**

Support one another every day. Help each other by sharing the necessities of life. Remind one another to be thankful to the Creator and observe the ceremonies.

6. **How did the Clan structure help build a sense of community?**

It created family relations that were obligated to help one another. Heron Clan helped Heron Clan within a particular nation but did not exclude interacting with other Clans in other nations.

7. **What do you think a person would do if they saw one of their Clan members being bullied or struggling to learn something?**

They would help them by trying to create a peaceful solution failing that by removing them from danger and protecting them.

	Hawk	Bear	Wolf	Turtle	Heron	Snipe	Deer	Beaver	Eel
Mohawk		X	X	X					
Seneca	X	X	X	X	X	X	X	X	
Oneida		X	X	X					
Onondaga	X	X	X	X	X	X	X	X	X
Cayuga		X	X	X	X	X			
Tuscarora		X	X	X			X	X	X

* Shaded area depicts the **Clans common** to all the Haudenosaunee (Six Nations) People

Can you identify the 9 Clan animals prints?

The 9 Clan animals prints identified.

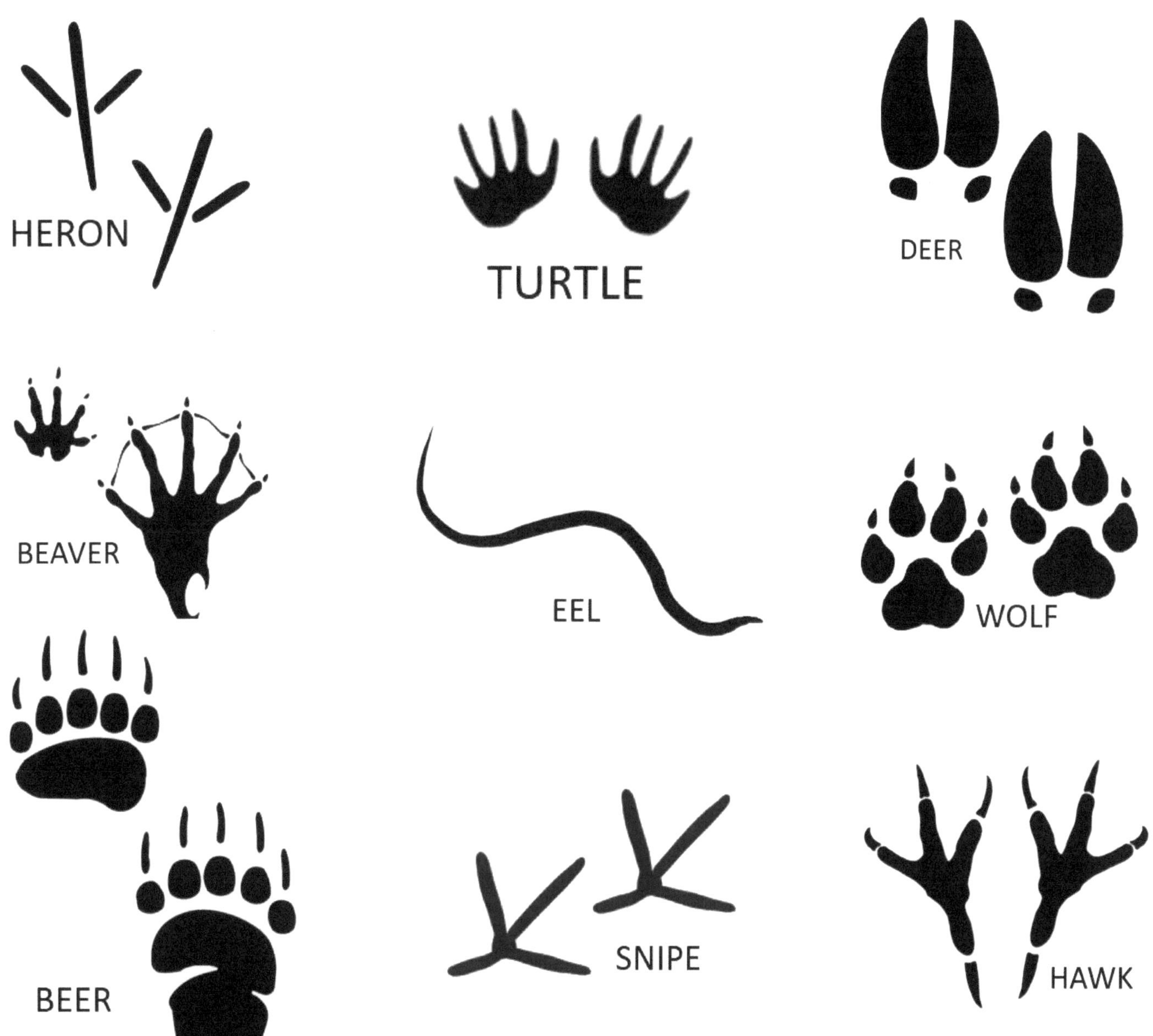

Colouring Activity

Artist's Name:

Zig Misiak arrived in Canada as a WW2 Polish baby refugee with his parents, Stanislaus and Zina Misiak in 1950. Over several decades, living in Brantford, he embraced and cultivated an interest in his neighbors, and friends, the Haudenosaunee, the Grand River Six Nations People.

Queen Elizabeth ll Diamond Jubilee Medal
Sovereign's Medal
Lieutenant Governor's Ontario Heritage Life-time achievement award
Polish Army Gold Medal—First Class
Polish Combatants' Bronze Cross
Shining Star Award
George & Olive Seibel Award
Inductee: Ancaster High School Hall of Distinction
Canadian Aboriginal Veterans Association Medallion

A Canadian Forces Veteran, RHLI, 1964-1969, a historic re-enactor: Roger's Rangers of the French and Indian Wars, Butler's Rangers of the American Revolution, Caldwell's Rangers of the War of 1812 as well as an active member of the SPK, Polish Combatant's Association and Royal Canadian Legion.

Jennifer Bettio, born and raised in Guelph Ontario, is an arts and photography graduate of Sheridan College. With support of her parents she pursued her interests in the arts field that has brought her great success. She does commissioned paintings, art, graphics and design, advertising, illustrations and unique photography. Her French Canadian Métis background, allows her to exhibit a unique First Nations and Métis style of art.